BRITAIN IN OLD PHO

THE LINCOLNSHIRE COAST

DAVID CUPPLEDITCH

SUTTON PUBLISHING LIMITED

Sutton Publishing Limited
Phoenix Mill · Thrupp · Stroud
Gloucestershire · GL5 2BU

First published 1996

Cover photographs: front: Baptists from Louth
enjoying a picnic in the dunes between
Mablethorpe and Saltfleetby, August 1870;
back: Kiddies' Corner, Mablethorpe, 1920s

British Library Cataloguing in Publication Data
A catalogue record for this book is available from the
British Library.

ISBN 0-7509-0699-5

Typeset in 10/12 Perpetua.
Typesetting and origination by
Sutton Publishing Limited.
Printed in Great Britain by
Ebenezer Baylis, Worcester.

Mablethorpe floods, 1953. On hand to dole out tea to emergency helpers who cleaned up the mess is this
group of volunteers. The ambulance is standing by, but the most important vehicle is the NAAFI wagon!

CONTENTS

All along this coast many sailors and swimmers have been thankful for the lifeboats. This is the *Heywood*, presented by Mr Heywood Lonsdale in 1883 and stationed in Mablethorpe.

A fishing tournament at Boston, *c.* 1910.

INTRODUCTION

The Lincolnshire coast is one of the few places left in Britain where there is a peaceful feeling of solitude. Because of its open spaces this shoreline makes an ideal venue for anyone wanting to escape the hustle and bustle of modern day life and 'recharge their batteries'. There is mile upon mile of lonely salt-marsh, sand-dune and shrub only a stone's throw away from the busy resorts of Cleethorpes, Mablethorpe, Sutton and Skegness. Here there is room to breathe, there is serenity, and it is often bracing!

The writer of a travel book published in Edwardian times summed it up when he said;

> The characteristics of the coast scenery of Skegness, Sutton-on-Sea and Mablethorpe are so similar that a description of one would serve for the other two. In each place there is a magnificent stretch of clean and firm sands, with a line of sandhills stretching on and on for miles in either direction between the shore and the bordering farm-lands. These hillocks, clothed in part by grass and plants, afford cosy resting nooks and shelters from sun or wind, and are scarcely inferior to the sands themselves as an attraction to visitors.

Many years later, D.H. Lawrence visited Mablethorpe and Skegness on holiday and indeed many Lincolnshire place-names can be found in his novels.

The area has also played host to royalty. HRH Princess Anne visited the East Coast on 15 September 1993, when she opened the new primary school at North Somercotes. She also visited the Willoughby Group of Riding for the Disabled near Alford, and fitted in a trip to Theddlethorpe on that same busy morning.

Historically this coastline is a combination of floods, sea defences, erosion, reclamation, smugglers and shipwrecks. Five medieval churches have been swallowed up by the sea and the flood of 1571 prompted Jean Ingelow to pen her famous poem 'The High Tide on the Coast of Lincolnshire'. In 1953 a total of 233 people died as a result of the Great East Coast Flood, thirty-five of whom died in Mablethorpe and Sutton. But the most notable reminder of the past lies in Fishtoft where the roadsign points to 'SCALP' and 'CUT END'. Down this road on the bank of The Haven lies Pilgrims' Pillar (erected in 1957) as Fishtoft's memorial to the Pilgrim Fathers.

It was from here that the Pilgrim Fathers first set sail for America in 1607. They were betrayed by their ship's captain, arrested and brought back to Boston in open boats where they were ridiculed as a 'spectacle and a wonder to the multitude'. Imprisoned in the medieval Guildhall for attempting to emigrate illegally, they eventually fled to Holland and later formed part of the group that sailed in the *Mayflower* from Southampton in 1620. Ten years later a further group set sail from Boston and founded the city of Boston, Massachusetts.

From Frieston shore to Wainfleet Sand there are dangerous mud flats from where the terms 'fen-slodger' and 'gozzard' originate. But from Gibraltar Point to Cleethorpes there is an almost uninterrupted stretch of fine golden sand. In the Great Exhibition of the 1920s, tons of Mablethorpe sand were transported to Wembley for use in displays. Nor is this coastline devoid of vegetation. The Victorian delicacy samphire, which Mrs Beeton used to pickle, grows in abundance.

At one time the Lincolnshire coast was well known for oysters and shellfish. And indeed my earliest memory of a visit to Anderby Creek in the fifties digging for cockles is imprinted on my mind forever. It was autumn, I was cold and hypothermia nearly set in. The typhoid epidemic at the turn of the century killed off the old oyster trade, while pollution in the North Sea has done much damage to shrimping and lobster fishing. Despite this heavy pollution, grey seals still return to Donna Nook every year in late November/early December to give birth to their pups. The dunes are covered with mothers and their young while the fathers or large bulls wait close by.

Many famous people in the field of entertainment have been born along this coast. Arthur Lucan (better known as 'Ole Mother Riley') was born in Boston, Elizabeth Allan, the Hollywood actress, was born in Skegness, and the late Patrick Wymark and Patricia Hodge count themselves as 'Meggies', which, translated, means they were Cleethorpes born. Numerous stars and personalities have appeared, both at the Embassy and at Cleethorpes pier, fulfilling the role which the Clements carried out for a number of years.

Everyone has their own memories of sea-side holidays, whether it be ice-cream, donkey rides or penny slot machines. Some of us can look back with nostalgia at those days, where the smell of ozone intermingled with the smell of fish and chips and vinegar! The sound of children's laughter was only interrupted by waves or squawking gulls circling overhead. Ultimately you recall the freedom far removed from road rage, stress and the Heath Robinson bureaucracy we all live with today, and you think 'Ah, those were the days'.

David Cuppleditch
1996

SECTION ONE

BOSTON

Boston, or Botolphstown, is the start of this journey along the Lincolnshire coast. In this photograph of boats on the Witham, the paddle steamer SS *Privateer* is acting as a tug to one of the sailing craft leaving Boston port.

It is difficult to believe that in Norman and medieval times Boston's port was one of the chief commercial ports in England, trading with ports in Northern Europe, Flanders and the Rhineland.

When Boston Dock was enlarged in 1882, at a cost of £170,000, the Mayor and his wife, Mr and Mrs J. Simmonds, cut the first sod. Looking on, with plans rolled up, is William Wheeler, Borough Surveyor.

Three mills used to stand on what is now the centre of Boston Dock. These are two of them. But all along the Lincolnshire coast lies a graveyard of this once flourishing trade.

Of the few remaining mills, and one in working order, is the Maude Foster Mill erected for Thomas and Isaac Reckitt in 1819. The name of Reckitt is retained in the successful company of Reckitt & Colman.

The familiar and distinctive features of the paddle tug SS *Privateer*, which travelled all around the Wash taking parties of people from Skegness pier to places as far away as Hunstanton. This photograph was taken at Packhorse Quay.

When John Rennie's Boston bridge was pulled down in April 1913 the SS *Privateer* was called upon to help demolish it. Sadly this friendly little tug was sunk in 1914 in the first days of the First World War while towing off France. John Rennie achieved wider fame as the designer of Waterloo Bridge in London.

This was how Boston Dock looked at the turn of the century, when timber was the major import.

And this is how it looked in the '50s, still importing timber!

Of course the familiar landmark all around is the Stump, which has acted as a beacon to many ships. The last vicar was the Revd Peter Fluck (brother of the late Diana Dors), who retired in 1995.

An earlier vicar was A.M. Cook (1931–46) who wrote his short history of Boston; this became so popular that it was reprinted in 1948. Later Cook became Sub-Dean of Lincoln Cathedral (1946–61).

Just in front of the Stump in the Market Place is a statue of Herbert Ingram, founder of the *Illustrated London News* in 1842.

The Guildhall in South Street (next to Fydell House and currently a museum) is the building in which the Pilgrim Fathers were imprisoned. (They eventually got away in the *Mayflower* in 1620.) Incidentally, the ivy has been removed from Fydell House since this photograph was taken.

Since the days of the Pilgrim Fathers Boston has retained strong links with the USA. In 1630 seven ships sailed under the Revd Isaac Johnson with such a preponderance of Boston men that Massachusetts' capital was given the town's name. In 1633 the famous preaching vicar John Cotton went there, and also Richard Bellingham, who became governor of Massachusetts. Here we see the Cotton Chapel in St Botolph's Church.

In the 1920s Sir Francis Fox visited the Stump and expressed his concern about the state of the tower. It was not until 1927, when the roof began to show alarming signs of decay, that the architect Sir Charles Nicholson was asked to report on the building. His report sparked off the massive restoration to which Boston, Massachusetts, gave £11,000; this was presented on 8 July 1931. The Stump is shown here when work was in progress.

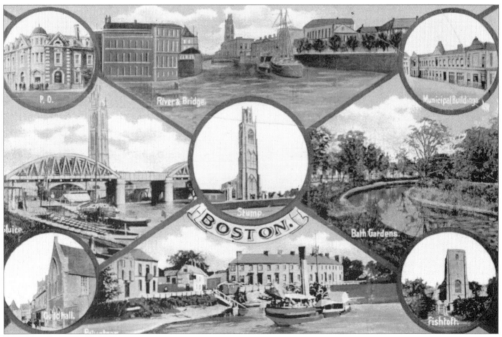

Of all the postcards produced, this composite probably provides the most comprehensive view of Boston.

The most prolific photographer in Boston in Victorian and Edwardian times was Hackford of Church Close.

The market is still as busy today as it was in Victorian times. This photograph was taken in about 1894.

Bostonians would always rise to the event. The celebration of Queen Victoria's Golden Jubilee in 1887 was marked by the roasting of an ox.

One landmark often overlooked and now rather neglected is the Hussey Tower (near Skirbeck Road). Lord Hussey was executed in 1541 at Lincoln for his part in the Lincolnshire Rebellion of 1536.

The Quay has changed somewhat with all the development that has taken place in Boston in recent years.

The Danish schooner *Frida*, the last sailing vessel to leave Boston Dock.

If this coast is a graveyard of former windmills the other casualty has been the parish church. Once the centre of every village, many of these churches now lie redundant. This is Fishtoft Church.

Butterwick Church has a fourteenth-century pulpit.

But if the parish church is in decline, local pubs seem to be on the up. This is The Barley Mow, Friskney, which thrives to this day although the name changed to The Witch and Cauldron in 1995.

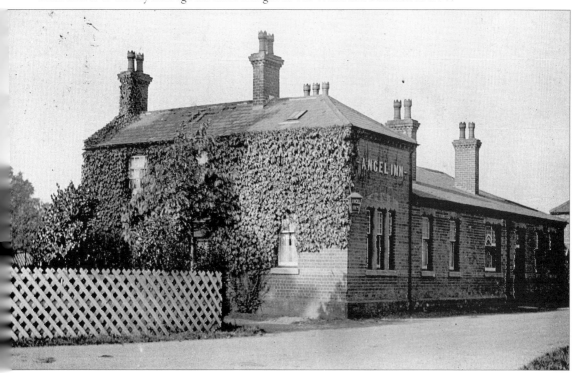

The nearby Angel Inn in Wrangle.

The popularity of hospitable drinking in public houses, especially in the south of the county, gave rise to the brewing family of Bateman's. They purchased Wainfleet All Saints' Mill and now use the windmill as their trademark. The weather vane on top of the mill carries the Bateman logo.

This was the original Salem Bridge Mill, Wainfleet, which was still operating as a mill until about 1920, shortly before the Bateman family bought it.

SKEGNESS

Near Skegness is the popular nature reserve of Gibraltar Point, now run by the Lincolnshire and South Humberside Trust for Nature Conservation.

The Jolly Fisherman poster, which appeared in 1908, advertised Great Northern Railway day trips at a cost of 3s from King's Cross to Skegness. The character has become synonymous with the town.

It would be difficult to think of Skegness without thinking of the word 'bracing' and vice versa. Yet its creator John Hassall received little financial reward. He was paid twelve guineas for his Jolly Fisherman poster and died in difficult circumstances in 1948. Hassall, seen here in his other favourite guise of amateur thespian, was made a Freeman of the Town in 1936.

The problem with Hassall was that he was an artist with a sense of humour, as can be seen in this follow-up poster stating: 'For all the ills we have to bear, There's nothing cures like East Coast air. It is SO bracing.'

The other man who did so much to put Skegness on the map was Billy Butlin, seen here in 1937 outside his holiday camp. It was Butlin who persuaded John Hassall to visit Skegness in 1936.

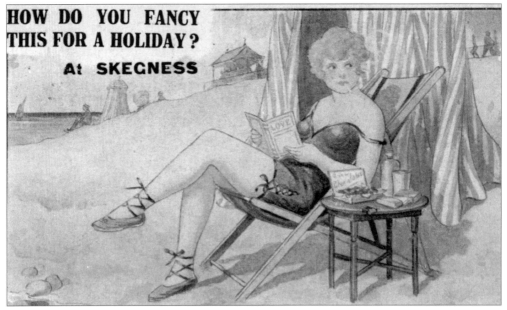

The postcard market flourished in the Edwardian era. Scantily clad mademoiselles enticed lustful young men on to the beach in the hope of catching a glance of ankle, or perhaps a bit more? Cards like this were sent in their thousands and paved the way for the more risqué joke cards that still sell today.

The big advantage that Skegness had was that it owned its own pier. Built in 1881, with Australian Jarrah decking and stout ironwork by Head, Wrightson & Co. of Teesdale, it was to remain a popular feature until 1978 when high winds and gales blew two sections down and wrecked it.

Another amusement was the *Eliza*, a two-masted ship (on the right of this postcard), which was beached and used as a museum.

Many families enjoyed having their photograph taken on the pier. This was the Hall Family from Louth. Just visible in the background is the makeshift diving board that 'Pegleg Gadsby' used to dive off for entertainment.

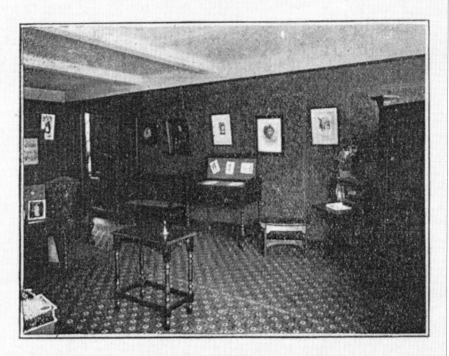
Capturing everything on camera was Wrate, the Skegness photographer whose studio was at 17 Lumley Road. It has often puzzled me why no one has ever compiled a dictionary of Lincolnshire photographers. Those who specialised in seaside scenes included Nainby of Alford, Bundock of Spilsby and Camm of Mablethorpe.

Charabanc parties flocked into Skegness for day trips.

Charabanc parked in front of the clock tower. Pevsner described the Jubilee Clock Tower of 1899 as architecturally negligible with a Big Ben top.

But there was still plenty for the day-tripper, including The Rock Gardens . . .

. . . or the Boating Lake, opened in 1924, which was such a success that it was extended two years later.

The swimming pool was also popular. When it opened in 1928 the bathing pool, with its twin chutes and diving boards, was the biggest on the East Coast, and was known as the New Wonder Pool of the East Coast.

Then there were the sands, with plenty of windbreakers to counteract that bracing wind.

This would have been the view most day-trippers would have seen if they had arrived at Skegness by train, looking down Lumley Road with the Lion Hotel on the left and Barlows on the right.

At the end of Lumley Road, just beside the clock tower, Les Howe (the Louth photographer) and family arrive for a day on the beach. Curiously enough, this was one of Wrates' walking photographs; it shows Clements Theatre in the background.

This is the clock tower, with Clements Theatre clearly visible in the middle of the photo.

For the more discerning there were two golf clubs in Skegness. One was at the North End, and this was the club house, now the North Shore Hotel.

The other golf club was based at the Vine Hotel. Known for a time as Enderby's Hotel, it still enjoys a good reputation. Tennyson is reputed to have played skittles here.

Only a short distance away is Coronation Walk, named after Edward VII's coronation in 1901. Coronation Walk started in Drummond Road and ran on to Richmond Drive, linking up with the Vine Hotel at Vine Walk.

Skegness probably enjoyed its heyday in those mid-war years of the '20s and '30s. There was a walk along the pier or, for the more adventurous, boat trips from the end of the pier.

This was the entrance to the Piazza Bathing Pool (now the Embassy), with its bandstand where holidaymakers could sit and enjoy the sunshine in deckchairs while listening to military brass band melodies. (Ah! Those were the days before portable radios or, even worse, ghetto-blasters!)

It must have been difficult for those pioneers who helped to put Skegness on the map, such as John Hassall or Billy Butlin, or even Skegness Corporation, to envisage this scene. Looking north towards Ingoldmells, there are row upon row of caravans clustered around Butlin's Fun Coast World holiday camp.

Hidden away off Church Road North and Lincoln Road is the delightful church of St Clement's.

Like so many towns and villages on this coast Skegness is the combination of a seaside resort mixed with a farming community. Even today there are no fewer than three working farms in Skegness, with one in the form of a museum – Church Farm Museum (off Church Road, and opened to the public in 1976). Within the museum grounds there is an example of an eighteenth-century mud and stud Lincolnshire labourer's cottage, which was removed from Witham and re-erected here in about 1980.

The labourer's cottage was based on this sort of dwelling, which once was so commonplace along this coast. Joseph Willey (the Louth photographer) took this photograph in the Grainthorpe/Mablethorpe area in about 1870.

There is also a blacksmith's workshop within the museum, which once again reminds us that there were hundreds of blacksmiths dotted throughout Lincolnshire. This is a typical photograph of nearby Revesby.

At nearby Gunby Hall can be seen the style in which some families lived before the advent of the dreaded bungalow. Long the seat of the Massingberd family, Gunby Hall was handed over to the National Trust by Sir Archibald Montgomery Massingberd in 1944, when this photograph was taken. It is open to the public from April to September.

For the elderly or middle-aged there was a game of bowls on North Parade.

By the 1930s the Jolly Fisherman had become the symbol of Skegness. It was the town's lucky charm, and reproductions of the Falstaffian character appeared on postcards, ash-trays, pottery and petrol caps! Despite the connection between Skegness and its Jolly Fisherman, a flood of postcards produced in the late '40s and '50s appeared with cats proposing a different kind of symbol.

It was almost as if Skegness had become intoxicated with the Jolly Fisherman and decisions had been made through an alcoholic haze. Fortunately the cat fad did not last long, and Skegness reverted to its dear old Jolly Fisherman once more.

SUTTON-ON-SEA

From Skegness to Mablethorpe the sea defences are constantly reviewed. This is part of the long-term Ham project, which involves building new defences and beach nourishment. The photo was taken at Mogg's Eye and shows dredgers in the background.

This sign shows how the revetment is added to existing sea defences that have reached the end of their life.

Sutton-on-Sea became so popular in Edwardian times that a travel writer was prompted to comment that 'it would not be surprising in the near future to see Sutton, as in Skegness, develop from a village into a town'. Here we see the promenade on the seafront, which stretched for a quarter of a mile when it was built in 1885.

The two principal hotels were the Bacchus (once known as the Jolly Bacchus) …

… and the Beach Hotel (now demolished). It is just visible in the background of this 1956 photograph.

Close to the old railway station was St Clement's Church, built in 1818 to replace the old medieval church which had slipped into the sea. Inside there is a stained glass memorial window to Bishop Bompas, first Bishop of the Yukon, commemorating his time as curate of this church.

The steam tramway that operated from Alford to Sutton, stopping at Bilsby, Markby and Hannah. It ran successfully for five years (1884–9).

Sutton station. When Sutton station opened in 1887, it effectively killed off the old steam tramway.

The chief attraction at Markby was the church with its thatched roof. The original roof was tiled, but in 1672 a churchwarden laid claim to the tiles in exchange for thatching the roof.

In 1908 some railway carriage bungalows were erected in Furlong Road. They were intended as temporary holiday cottages but all these years later are still standing and still used.

This is Waveland, one of the remaining cottages.

Throughout the '20s and '30s Sutton remained a popular resort, especially with children. This is one of the Howe children, wearing his dad's boots!

Bathing costumes could be a bit risqué!

Fashions change. This group of girls on Sutton beach in the early '50s would not have been seen dead in culottes in the '60s, but they are back in fashion in the 1990s.

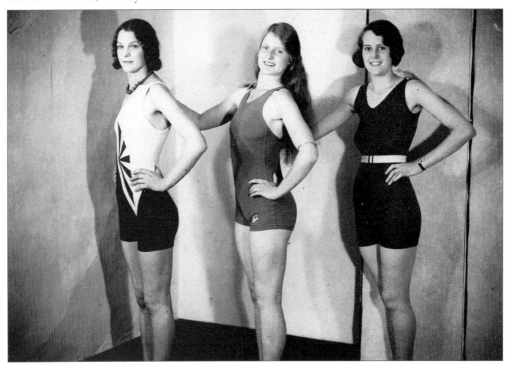

Mind you, swimsuits seem to get skimpier and skimpier. These were fashionable in the late '30s — the front one complete with sunburst motif.

A group of happy holidaymakers photographed in Sutton's old pleasure gardens in July 1952. These gardens were destroyed in the 1953 floods.

By August 1954 the pleasure gardens had been rebuilt and reopened. Here we see the Mayor, Revd Jack Parkinson, opening the Mapleleaf Pool, a gift from the people of Canada.

Hundreds of thousands of children have paddled in the Mapleleaf Pool. These two little girls are Maureen and Janet.

Because the damage caused by the 1953 flood was so extensive, the new sea defences had to be strong!

Hundreds of tons of concrete were poured into these defences which lined the East Coast. Much of the money came from government aid.

In Sutton new beach huts were built on top of the defences. With names like GCHQ, Wyworrie, Atonic and Sunbleste, these beach chalets differ from the old corrugated huts that used to stand in Sutton's Bohemia.

The Sandilands Golf Course had to be relaid.

Originally Sutton's War Memorial was erected on the promenade. In 1955 it was re-erected in the pleasure gardens.

This was the Mablethorpe and Sutton Eisteddfod of 1955, when Mr Houltby (the solicitor) presented the prizes. Also in the picture is a young Revd J.E. Swaby (author of *A History of Louth*).

For the remainder of the '50s Sutton enjoyed that post-war tranquil holiday atmosphere. This photograph was taken by Ken Atterby of Northgate Studios, Louth.

Providing entertainment today is this recently photographed Ladies Theatre Group . . .

. . . just as the Clements did so successfully in Mablethorpe and Skegness.

TRUSTHORPE

The mill at Trusthorpe was one of Lincolnshire's tallest mills comprising eight floors. It was built in 1881 to replace a post mill nearby.

Although it was working well into this century, modern technology forced it to close.

All that is left is the stump, which has been converted into a private house.

In the 1940s tall radio masts appeared and served as landmarks. Now known as BT Radio Humber, this radio station was so powerful it reached all parts of the globe.

Technology had been greatly accelerated during the Second World War and this enabled radio hams to talk from Hong Kong to South America at a time when telephone communication was restricted.

In 1871 the Convalescent Home between Trusthorpe and Mablethorpe was completed. The idea came from a Miss Emily Anderson, who saw the need to provide holidays for the underprivileged and those recuperating from non-infectious diseases in the Midland counties. The home was opened in June 1871 at a cost of £3,800, and James Fowler of Louth designed the building. Much of the money came from Canon Pretyman, a wealthy clergyman of Great Carlton.

In 1907 a children's wing was added, which enabled a further ten boys and ten girls to stay at the home.

Conditions inside the home were a bit spartan. This was the dining room.

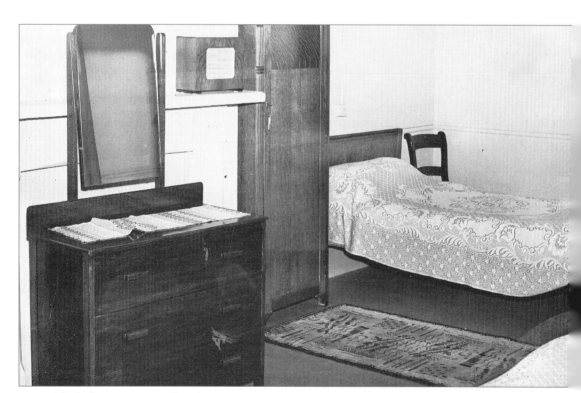

The bedrooms were very basic!

While the sea defences were being built in 1953, rough seas often hampered the work. The Convalescent Home was flooded in 1953, like so many homes along this shore. Rough seas often hampered the work of rebuilding the new defences.

Eventually the defences at Trusthorpe were completed in spring 1954.

The Convalescent Home closed in 1982, was demolished in 1987, and a block of luxury flats known as Queen's Park Close was erected on this site.

In complete contrast, the stumps of a submerged forest can be seen at low tide on this shore, as a reminder that this is an ever changing coastline.

MABLETHORPE

In this aerial shot of Mablethorpe the old Convalescent Home is visible in the bottom right-hand corner.

Like Sutton, Mablethorpe came to prominence in Edwardian times as a holiday retreat. This was a view of the booths and shacks that lined the beach.

Tennyson spent many of his youthful summer holidays in what was then a quiet seaside retreat. His seaside lodging was known locally as Ingoldby House, and was hidden behind some houses off Quebec Road. It was here in 1827 that Charles and Alfred Tennyson retired after their first book, *Poems by Two Brothers*, was published by Jackson's of Louth. Alfred Tennyson was so elated that he roamed the empty sandhills quoting from his own verses.

Pavilion and Sands, Mablethorpe.

The popularity of Mablethorpe as a resort can be seen in this Edwardian postcard, which shows the old lifeboat house on the right of the two helter-skelters, and Clements' entertainment booth in the centre.

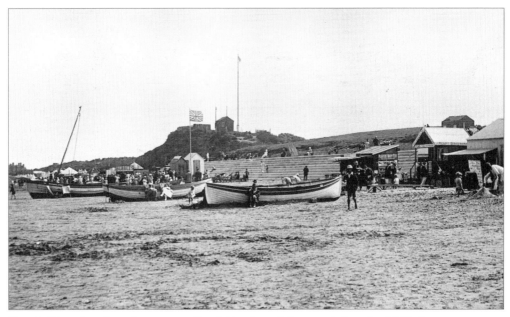

Even in Edwardian times there were a few fishing boats left to remind us that Mablethorpe was once a fishing village.

Postcards like this one were sent in their thousands, as the Edwardians loosened the tight corsets of Victorian suppression.

Most of the postcards produced for Mablethorpe reflect this image: donkeys, sun, sea and sand.

This is my favourite Mablethorpe postcard.

Clements the entertainers were a popular feature. They gave two concerts during the day on Mablethorpe beach and one evening performance in the Victoria Road Pavilion.

One of the notable features of the East Coast is the contrast between flat open sands and sky, as demonstrated by this photograph taken from Mablethorpe North End.

The Leicester Children's Holiday Home was started in 1898 by Lady Rolleston, wife of Sir John Rolleston, a well-known Leicester architect. The idea was to give Leicester's underprivileged children a two-week holiday. These holidays became extremely popular and highly sought after. By 1936 this building was erected to cope with the increase in demand. All these years later Englebert Humperdinck (the pop singer) is one of the patrons.

The promenade and pull-over, *c.* 1910.

With the advantage of a railway hundreds of people flocked to this resort. This was the pull-over which was often packed with folk during the summer months.

Bell tents were used for changing, and children enjoyed the freedom of fresh air and close supervision.

A 'kiddies' corner' was introduced on the beach with, just visible in the distance, the old wooden changing huts, which replaced the bell tents. On the top of the concrete steps was a hut known as 'The Old Man's Parliament'.

Once again we see the Louth photographer Les Howe with his two sons, this time sitting in front of the wooden changing huts (now demolished). H.L. Howe (1897–1959) was responsible for taking many of the photographs in this book.

Then there were the donkeys. The pork pie hut in the background has since been removed.

One of the popular attractions was this model railway which operated off High Street from about 1930 up to the Second World War. It was operated by Percy Harding-Kiff.

All along this coast caravans abound. Even in the '50s they were multiplying like rabbits. This was the view of North End. The advent of the caravan was the final nail in the coffin for Mablethorpe's railway, which closed in 1960, and many holidaymakers now towed their own private apartments on the back of their cars to their holiday destinations, much to the annoyance of local guesthouse owners and hotel keepers.

Because of the media coverage during the 1953 floods, Mablethorpe found itself at the centre of attention over the next few years. This was the Trade Fair held in 1954 with the Mayor, Revd Jack Parkinson, looking on.

When the new defences had been installed the Duke of Edinburgh came to inspect them on 14 February 1955. Once again Mayor Jack Parkinson was on hand to meet him. In the background are, left to right, Chief Constable Fowkes, Inspector Charlie Lewis and Sergeant Bray.

After that fateful day in January 1953 everyone had to work quickly before the next high tide in mid-February. Because of the fear of a repetition the Army was rushed to help, and a total of 700,000 tons of slag and rubble were transported from Scunthorpe to plug the gaps in the sea wall.

Even in the face of adversity Mablethorpe residents did not lose their sense of humour. The sign which had been placed in the lounge of a house in the Boulevard simply says 'concealed entrance'! In total an estimated 750,000 tons of sand had been deposited over the flooded area.

The damage that was caused can be seen in this photograph of South Promenade.

This is how it looked before the flood, with the old coastguard look-out hut clearly visible in the background.

Typical of so many homes, 'Sorrento' has its front sitting-room missing. The force of water blew a hole straight through the bungalow.

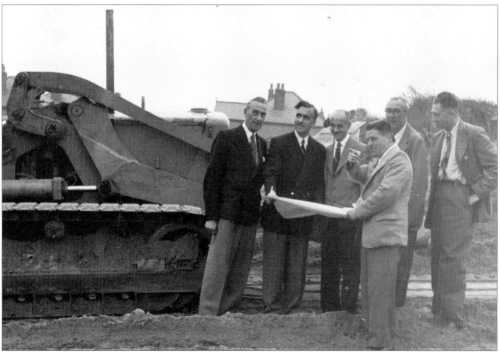

This was the team responsible for installing the new defences. The photograph was taken at Mablethorpe Sea Bank Park in 1955.

Part of the defence at the Point, Chapel St Leonards, also photographed in 1955.

Hundreds of tons of rubble were deposited all along the coast, and lorries worked day and night to fill the gaps.

People flocked to Mablethorpe, as can be seen by this crowd which came to watch the 1954 Grand Carnival.

Floats were paraded through the town.

Part of the publicity drive to attract more visitors to Mablethorpe in 1955 included this van, which was used as a mobile information unit.

Wilfred Pickles brought his 'Have a Go' radio programme to Mablethorpe in December 1955.

That summer one of the more bizarre spectacles on the beach was an elephant!

These two young girls are enjoying a ride on the old amusements. The dodgem track is in the background.

Roads were widened to make way for increased traffic, such as this road improvement of North End in 1955.

Visitors used to love having their photograph taken on holiday as a souvenir; these were called 'walking photographs'. The two photographers who did much work in the Mablethorpe area were Wrates of Skegness and W. Camm. This is a charming example of Wrates' walking photographs, dated 8 September 1947.

While this is an example of W. Camm's 'Souvenir of a Happy Holiday', taken in the late '50s. The little girl in this snapshot is called Pamela.

A Darby and Joan Christmas party, also photographed by W. Camm & Son of Royal Studios, High Street, 1955.

Old Mr Brownlow spent his lifetime collecting for charity. Here he is pictured outside the Brownlow bungalows with his pram. During the Second World War he collected enough money to pay for two Spitfires!

This was Mablethorpe Primary School in the early '50s.

SALTFLEETBY & THEDDLETHORPE

The first lifeboat station was established at Theddlethorpe in 1829, moving to Mablethorpe in 1883. Simply manoeuvring the boat into the water was an arduous task. Here we see the *John Rowson Lingard* being lifted into the water with the aid of pulleys, carthorses and plenty of strong lifeboatmen.

When the *John Rowson Lingard* was launched in 1905 by Baroness von Eckarstein, crowds of people flocked to Mablethorpe to watch the ceremony.

Many ships have floundered on this coast. This was the *Emma*, a two-masted barque which came to grief off Mablethorpe in 1902. It was used as a marine museum for a time before being broken up, and its timbers used to prop up the Basin.

In 1907 the *Hera* also came to grief in very nearly the same spot. This time its timbers were used in the walls of the pull-over.

After the *Prussian Queen* floundered off Saltfleetby and was wrecked, its timbers were used in the construction of the present Prussian Queen pub, whose football team is pictured here. Nearby Donna Nook was also named after a ship that was wrecked on this shore.

In 1878 the *Donna Nook* lifeboat was captured on canvas, the painting conveying some of the difficulties lifeboatmen had to experience. In the 1840s a Donna Nook farmer called Richard Hoodless swam his horse through the stormy sea to save four men from a wreck the lifeboat could not reach. He was awarded the silver medal from the Royal Human Society for his bravery.

Even Rimac was named after a brig which was wrecked on this coast in 1874, while on its way from Constadt to Kingston-upon-Hull.

These days Rimac is a nature reserve, and the only place in Lincolnshire where wild orchids can be found. Here we see two workmen repairing steps on the sanctuary. The cost of upkeep is borne by English Heritage and English Nature.

Not all the vessels that floundered on this coast with its shifting sandbanks became wrecks. Here we see a two-masted barque that ran aground off Saltfleetby in the '20s, only to be refloated on the next available high tide.

All along this coast fishermen and anglers can enjoy their sport. There are numerous dykes, ponds and rivers, the banks of which are packed with fishermen during the summer months. This photograph was taken at Vicker's Pond, Saltfleetby, on 28 July 1949.

Most people who lived on this coast enjoyed the 'good life' of self sufficiency and organically grown crops. This was the Bett family of Saltfleetby, who were obviously proud of their chickens.

Saltfleet Manor House is steeped in history. Oliver Cromwell is said to have slept here after the Battle of Winceby.

Downstairs there is a panel behind which Cromwell was supposed to have been concealed.

The annual sale of foals which took place every October has long since ceased. This was Mr Chambers, a grey colt who won the Franklin cup for best foal in the 1935 show.

Despite the disappearance of the foal show, this stretch of coast is still suitable for exercising horses. These horse trials took place at nearby Manby.

Of the three churches in Saltfleetby, Saltfleetby All Saints' is the most unusual. The leaning tower is now leaning even more and the roof over the nave looks as if it is about to break in two. Much of the inside dates from the fifteenth century and it is well worth a visit.

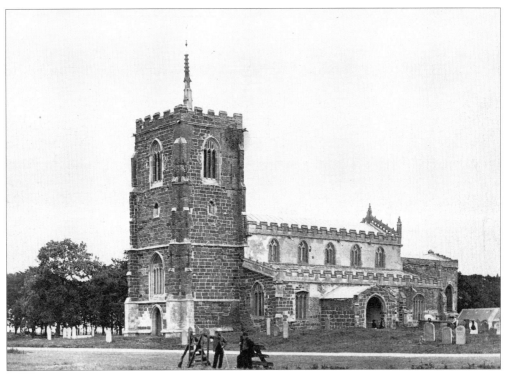

Like so many of these East Coast churches, both Saltfleetby All Saints' and nearby Theddlethorpe All Saints' (shown here) are now redundant. Theddlethorpe was nicknamed the 'cathedral of the marshes'.

All Saints' Mill, Theddlethorpe, *c.* 1911. The mill was later demolished.

But if Theddlethorpe Mill is a reminder of the past, there is hope for the future in Theddlethorpe Primary School. Here we see the children as they prepare for the Big Banana Show on children's television in 1991.

The North Somercotes pancake race is one of the highlights of the village year. Started in 1954 by Lt Col G.S. Grey, it takes place on Shrove Tuesday. Here we see the winner and runner-up on 14 February 1956.

Originally the pancake race was held between residents of North Somercotes and a village in Sussex. Now it is a popular local event, especially with children.

Just as Clarke's ice-creams were well known in the area at the turn of the century, now it is Appleby's. Their headquarters in Conisholme has an ice-cream shop and tea-room. The firm, which also specialises in coach trips and travel, has blossomed in recent years.

At a time when most chapels are left derelict and disused, Conisholme Chapel has had an extension and has been renovated.

The chapel at Marshchapel has been recently restored and now serves as a community centre.

The church in Marshchapel is a particularly fine Perpendicular example of the fifteenth-century church building. The treble bell, re-cast in 1919, bears the names of eight Marshchapel men who died in the First World War. Its bells ring out over some 600 acres of salt 'fitties' reclaimed for Marshchapel and Grainthorpe from the sea.

CLEETHORPES

Cleethorpes enjoyed a good reputation as a seaside resort in Victorian and Edwardian times. This was the slipway to the sea in about 1905.

A favourite pastime with holidaymakers was to hire a boat, which would then have to be dragged into the Humber for an enjoyable trip on the water.

Like Skegness, Cleethorpes had the advantage of a pier which had the pavilion right at the end of it. This photograph was taken from the Cliff Hotel.

On 6 July 1903 disaster struck when the pier caught fire and collapsed. The end-of-pier pavilion was replaced with a new pavilion at the pier entrance.

The Cliff Hotel, which opened in 1863, offered generous hospitality at a price. The building has long ceased to be a hotel and is currently a night club.

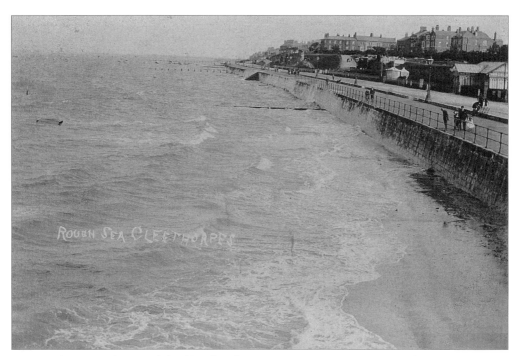

Because Cleethorpes lay on soft boulder clay, there was constant erosion. In 1902 the houses that faced the sea on Sea Bank road (now Kingsway) lay in danger of falling into the sea. Concrete defences were built to prevent this from happening.

With trams that regularly ran to and from Grimsby, the resort lay within easy reach for most Grimbarians to partake of fresh sea air. Just visible is the cast-iron fountain that marked Queen Victoria's Diamond Jubilee.

Before it was removed to Kingsway the fountain was erected on the sea front. Sadly it was demolished in 1949, and an old landmark disappeared.

Another landmark which has disappeared is the statue of the Boy with the Leaking Boot, originally donated to Cleethorpes by a Swedish Consul, John Carlbom.

The Boy with the Leaking Boot was to Cleethorpes what the Jolly Fisherman was to Skegness. Unfortunately it suffered all forms of vandalism before it was finally removed.

Even on those dreadful postcards of the '50s and '60s he is featured as a symbol of the town.

Throughout the '20s and '30s Cleethorpes built on its reputation as a fun-loving resort. This was the kiddies' sandpit at Thrunscoe recreation ground.

Members of the Howe family have turned up again, this time at the side of the sandpit enjoying a typical day out.

The boating lake . . .

. . . and once again Les Howe, the Louth photographer, and Marion, his wife, are back in the picture.

As hundreds of day-trippers flocked to Cleethorpes, businesses grew and money flooded into the resort.

Trees matured around the boating lake and it was enlarged.

When Cleethorpes became a Borough,
Mayor Councillor Sir George Moody JP
accepted the Charter in 1936.

It was presented to him by Lord Heneage,
who also gave the town its cenotaph in 1919.

One distinctive reminder of the art deco period is the Electricity showroom on Isaac Hill.

By the 1950s deckchairs were in demand on Cleethorpes beach, and parking became something of a problem.

The old Wonderland with its big dipper, dodgems and carousel has been replaced with amusement arcades, Fantasy World, bingo parlours and fish and chip shops.

Cleethorpes, like Sutton, Mablethorpe and Skegness, was affected by the 1953 flood. This is a view of the promenade strewn with debris.

Young army recruits were called in to help clear up the mess in Cleethorpes, just as the group of volunteers below had helped out in Mablethorpe.

St Peter's Church owes its existence to the boundless energy of the Revd William Price Jones, who was appointed to Clee-cum-Cleethorpes in 1850 at the age of twenty-nine. William Price Jones also organised the building of the vicarage (now part of Church School) and helped to carve some of the stonework in the south wall.

The man in the moon took over as a symbol of the town.
Here we see the lights being switched on in 1979 by
Mayor Winn.

Cleethorpes has its own model railway, the Cleethorpes Coast Light Railway. This is Chris Shaw, the
owner, taking it for a trial run.

Undoubtedly one of the most celebrated events is the Cleethorpes Carnival, held during the last weekend in July. Here we see some revellers outside The Fisherman's Arms in Seaview Street.

In charge of the donkeys is that popular couple Stanley and Gladys Nuttall. This photograph was taken in 1990, when Gladys was Mayor of Cleethorpes.

The Lincolnshire coast is primarily a fun area for children. This photograph was taken at the opening of the new Leisure Centre in Cleethorpes in 1990.

It has indoor sporting facilities and a heated swimming pool. This is the paddling pool for the very young children.

Nearby is the ever popular Pleasure Island.

The Point, Chapel St Leonards. When an angry sea lashes against the fine basketwork breakwater it presents a wonderful sight.

ACKNOWLEGEMENTS

There are many people whom I would like to thank for helping me to put this slim volume together, most notably Peter Chambers, Norman Cawkwell, Ben Jacklin, Charles Smith, Geoffrey Roe, Brian Howe and Ken Atterby for allowing me to borrow certain photographs. A special thank you must go to Peter Moore, editor of the *Grimsby Evening Telegraph*, for allowing me to reproduce one or two photos from their archives, and I am extremely indebted to Janet Longden, Peter Chapman and Peter Craig (from the *Grimsby Evening Telegraph*) for their time and patience, not forgetting Louth Secretarial Services who typed this manuscript so carefully.

BRITAIN IN OLD PHOTOGRAPHS

To order any of these titles please telephone our distributor, Littlehampton Book Services on 01903 721

For a catalogue of these and our other titles please ring Regina Schinner on 01453 731114